Otherlands

Also by Harry Guest

Poetry
A Different Darkness
Arrangements
The Cutting-Room
The Achievements of Memory
Mountain Journal
A House Against the Night
The Hidden Change
Lost and Found
Coming to Terms
So Far
A Puzzling Harvest (*Collected Poems 1955–2000*)
Comparisons & Conversions *
Some Times

Novels
Days
Lost Pictures
Time After Time

Radio Plays
The Inheritance
The Emperor of Outer Space

Translations
Post-War Japanese Poetry (*with Lynn Guest and Kajima Shôzô*)
The Distance, The Shadows (*66 Poems by Victor Hugo*)
Versions
From a Condemned Cell (*33 Sonnets by Jean Cassou*)
A Square in East Berlin (*a novel by Torsten Schulz*)

Non-Fiction
Another Island Country
Mastering Japanese
Traveller's Literary Companion to Japan
The Artist on the Artist

* *published by Shearsman Books*

Otherlands

Translations of
Jean Cassou,
Rainer Maria Rilke
& other poets

by

Harry Guest

Shearsman Books

First published in the United Kingdom in 2017 by
Shearsman Books
50 Westons Hill Drive
Emersons Green
BRISTOL
BS16 7DF

Shearsman Books Ltd Registered Office
30–31 St. James Place, Mangotsfield, Bristol BS16 9JB
(this address not for correspondence)

www.shearsman.com

ISBN 978-1-84861-479-6

Translations copyright © Harry Guest, 2008, 2017.

Copyright in these translations remains with Harry Guest, who has asserted his right to be identified as the translator of these works, in accordance with the Copyrights, Designs and Patents Act of 1988. All rights reserved.

We are grateful to:
Editions Gallimard and the Estate of Jean Cassou for permission to reprint the poems by Jean Cassou from *Trente-trois sonnets composés au secret*, Jean Cassou © Editions Gallimard, Paris, 1995;

Rowohlt Verlag for Rolf Dieter Brinkmann, 'Selbstbildnis im Supermarkt'; 'Noch mehr Schatten', from: Rolf Dieter Brinkmann, *Standphotos. Gedichte 1962-1970* Copyright © 1980 Rowohlt Verlag GmbH, Reinbek bei Hamburg;

Insel Verlag, Berlin, for 'Nicht gesagt' and 'Spiralen' by Marie-Luise Kaschnitz, from *Gesammelte Werke in sieben Bänden, Band 5: Die Gedichte*, copyright © Insel Verlag, Frankfurt am Main 1985. All rights controlled through and reserved by Insel Verlag Berlin.

The poems by Rolf Haufs, Anne Mounic and Daniele Serafini are published here by kind permission of the authors.

Some of the translations collected here originally appeared in *Agenda, The Broadsheet, Fortnightly Review, HQ Poetry, The Menard Press, Modern Poetry in Translation, PN Review, Shearsman* magazine and *Sofia*.

Contents

Clément Marot
    About My Self   9

Mellin de Saint-Gelais
    Sonnet   10

Maurice Scève
    from Délie, dizain no. CCXVI   11
    dizain no. CCLVII   12
    To the Reader   13

Olivier de Magny
    "Holà Charon..."   14

Joachim du Bellay
    Sonnet LXXVI from *L'Olive*   16

Philippe Desportes
    Sonnet LI from *Les Amours d'Hippolyte*   17
    "Love can at the same moment
    goad and check"   18

Théophile Gautier
    Preface to *Emaux et Camées*   19

Stéphane Mallarmé
    Breeze off the Sea   20
    Renewal   21
    Anguish   22

Paul Verlaine
    Monsieur Bourgeois   23

Arthur Rimbaud
    Ah seasons   Ah castles   24
    The Flags of May   25
    Seascape   26

Rainer Maria Rilke
    Endymion   27
    Childhood   28
    People by Night   30
    The Mount of Olives   31
    The Lay of the Love and Death of
        Cornet Christoph Rilke von Langenau   33

Marie Luise Kaschnitz
    Spirals   45
    Unsaid   46

Rolf Haufs
    Peppino Portiere   47

Rolf-Dieter Brinkmann
    Self-Portrait in the Supermarket   48
    Even More Shadows   49

Jean Cassou
    33 Sonnets composed in secret   51
    Notes to the 33 Sonnets   86

Anne Mounic
    "the duel now more one-sided than before"   90
    "arresting sleights of hand"   91
    "infinity, conceivable florescence"   92

Daniele Serafini
    A Distant Venice   93

Ryôta
        Haiku   97

Harry Guest
        Ryôta's Twilit Haiku   98

        Six Word-Sonnets   100

Harry Guest
        Quantité Inconnue   102

Notes on the Poets   104

Clément Marot
(1495-1544)

About My Self   *[De Soy Mesme]*

I'm not now what I used to be
and can't bring lost time back to me.

Those lovely Aprils flew out through
the window, those sweet summers too.

Neglecting other gods I know
I served my master Eros though

if he could get me born once more
I'd serve him better than before

Mellin de Saint-Gelais
(1487-1558)

Sonnet

Watching that range of distant mountains I
compare it to the length of my distress;
those peaks are lofty, my desire as high,
they stand there firm, my faith's as serious.
So many glittering brooks stream down their side.
From my eyes tears flow just as readily.
I cannot count how many times I've sighed.
Those summits suffer gales as ceaselessly.
A thousand flocks graze on those lower slopes.
As many loves are nurtured and reborn
inside my heart which fosters all my hopes
which bear no fruit. My joys have been withdrawn.
We're much alike. One feature's not the same –
in them the snow lasts, in me it's the flame.

Maurice Scève
(c.1510–c.1564)

from Délie, dizain no. CCXVI

At divers times, so many hours and days,
you come, my lady, to my soul to share
from hour to moment, moment to always,
the mesh of contradictions lurking there.
You live through calendars of mine which seem
exempt at least from minor grievances
while I, lost to reality in dread,
feel I have no-one but my self to please.
That's why I can't restrain the Furies by
will-power however ardently I try.

Délie *dizain* CCLVII

That mirror hanging always on its nail
needs daybreak to receive her image where
my heart in waiting daily must entail
false hoping that she'd like me with her there.
Your luck is such she often comes to see
you look at her knowing you won't betray
tears shed, complaints, what happens after. All
is secrecy since any woman may
get caught by you but if she's held in thrall
no-one can join her as a referee.

To the Reader

Scève's prologue to his long philosophical poem 'Microcosme'

A vain desire to visit various lands
brings kudos to the vagabond who strays
forfeiting much by switching skies and grounds.
More cautious use of years earns better days.

Time wasted gains approval from all those
who gape at new amazement which can reap
rewards won also by the ones who chose
to work – a verb to make the idle weep.

Thus wandering in sunlight I shall deign
to try both late and uselessly to please
not cup in hand to ask a different favour.

Thus lilies withered can flaunt blooms again
and autumn coaxing decorate fig-trees
with second fruit though green and lacking flavour.

    NOT HERE NOT THERE

Olivier de Magny
(d. 1560)

"Holà Charon..."
A Dialogue in Sonnet Form

<u>The Poet</u>
Hey! Charon! Yes, you, boatman of the dead.

<u>Charon</u>
Some bumptious ass is yelling. Who are you?

<u>The Poet</u>
The weeping spirit of a lover who
For faithfulness gained only tears to shed.

<u>Charon</u>
What do you want?

<u>The Poet</u>
    To cross the Styx to Hell.

<u>Charon</u>
You've killed a man?

<u>The Poet</u>
    That I have never done.
Love made me die.

<u>Charon</u>
    I can't take anyone
Who's gripped by love as though beneath a spell.

The Poet
Oh be a sport for once. Take me across.

Charon
Get someone else to row you. Neither I
Nor Fate would dare to disobey Eros.

The Poet
I'll go in spite of you. My soul has more
Tears for my eyes and loving tricks to try.
I'll be the river, be both boat and oar.

Joachim du Bellay
(1522-1560)

Sonnet LXXVI from *L'Olive*

When fierce storms scrape high hills and level ground
And rip her olive-tree from my poor heart
The famished wolf will lie down with the hound
Supposed to keep his flock safe and apart.

The pathway of that gale will sweep the skies
To emptiness, quenching their blue with dark.
Fires will give off no heat, no light. Those eyes
Of hers, once beautiful, will have no spark.

All creatures will exchange the lair they'd made
One with the other and the clearest noon
Resemble midnight at its bleakest. Soon

The colours of each field will seem the same,
The sea lack water, woods contain no shade
And roses lose the scent which lent them fame.

Philippe Desportes
(1546-1606)

Sonnet LI from *Les Amours d'Hippolyte*

The water dripping from a stalactite
Wears out the hardest marble and it's known
That diamonds melt in lion's blood despite
Resisting anvils and the flame. All stone –
Boulders – the granite cliff blocking the way –
Succumb when fire attacks the living rock.
North winds have toppled oak-trees you would say
Were old and tough enough to stand the shock.

But cursèd Eros sees how day and night
I spend my breath in sighing, my bruised eyes
Get drenched with tears, my soul's charred by my plight.
I find no way to soften the hard heart
Of one augmenting by her cruel art
My love for her, my sobs, my wounds, my sighs.

"Amour en mesme instant m'aiguillonne et m'arreste..."

Love can at the same moment goad and check,
Console and terrify, blaze up and freeze,
Pursue and flee, construct with care and wreck,
Crown me as victor, force me to my knees.

The plaything of the storm, tossed high, brought low,
I'm steered by Love erratically at will.
I feel secure awaiting the death-blow,
Believe I've won when I'm a loser still.

What pleased me once displeases me to-day.
I fall in love with her I don't desire.
Finding my heart's delight I'm led astray

And get entangled in protecting wire.
Knowing what can assist me in my plight
I move to act and fail to do what's right.

Théophile Gautier
(1811-1872)

The Preface to *Emaux et Camées*

Goethe ignored the brutal times
when empires made the cannons roar.
His *East-West Divan* (book of rhymes)
gave breathing-space for art to soar.

Shakespeare he spurned for Persian song,
perfumed himself with sandalwood
and borrowed metres which belong
to Middle-Eastern brotherhood.

Calm on his divan hour by hour,
aware those battles raged in vain,
he plucked a petal from each flower.

I wrote, although the hurricane
lashed windows which I always close,
Enamels first, then *Cameos*.

Stéphane Mallarmé
(1842-1898)

Breeze off the Sea *(Brise marine)*

Indulgence has I fear grown dismal now.
As for my books I've read them all. To flee's
the answer — far away! Swallows know how
to skim across the foam of unknown seas.
Nothing — no ancient garden mirrored by
her eyes can lure me from that spray, those skies,
nor lonely lamplight where my pages lie
unwritten on, too white — each warns, denies —
nor yet that baby at her mother's breast.
Somewhere's a ship with swaying masts. I'll leave
to seek another world, unfound, unguessed.
Bored, cruelly let down, I still believe
that handkerchiefs may flutter in farewell.
Masts can draw lightning, in the tempest all
be lost, no isle in sight, lost in the swell . . .
but in my soul I hear the sailors call!

Renewal

Spring sickly now with mourning drove away
the winter, lucid winter, when calm reigns
for art. Blood murky in my soul holds sway
but lengthy yawns prove impotence remains.

White twilights lose their warmth inside my head
clamped by an iron ring like some old tombstone.
Across fields where fecundity has spread
I'm left to track vague dreams, sweet ones, alone.

I drop exhausted by the scent of trees,
scoop out a ditch for false hopes with my jaw,
scrunch tepid earth where lilacs grow with ease

and wait to raise my boredom as disguise.
An azure brilliance alters leaves before
so many fledglings chirp at early skies.

Mallarmé named this 'Vere Novo' but altered the title to 'Renouveau' for publication in Parnasse Contemporain.

Anguish

I haven't come this night to vanquish one
who steals sins from her clients nor endure
such misery fingered through her hair. You've won
a kiss. My boredom's still beyond all cure.

From your bed I crave heavy sleep, no dreams.
Curtains conceal remorse. That's left unsaid,
sipped from dark lying. You must know, it seems,
far more of nothingness now than the dead.

Vice gnawing at the poise I'm pleased to own
has like you marked me with sterility.
Your bosom stone-like hides a heart so proud

no crime has left a fang-wound there while I
flee, pale, defeated, haunted by my shroud,
fearful of dying if I sleep alone.

Mallarmé called this 'A celle qui est tranquille'
and altered it later to 'Angoisse'.

Paul Verlaine
(1844-96)

Monsieur Bourgeois

He's grave, a family man, an alderman.
His collar's high and hides his ears. A pair
Of watery eyes see vaguely what they scan
And stitched flowers make his slippers nice to wear.

The stars mean nothing to him – nor the green
Meadows at dawn when sunlight flicks the dew –
Nor birds that sing at dusk and stay unseen.
He dreams of marrying off his daughter to

Young Monsieur Whatsit who is Croesus-rich.
He's middle-of-the-road, a botanist
And fat. As for those versifiers, those

Unshaven layabouts, long-haired, half-pissed,
He hates them like his ever-runny nose
And flowers grace his slippers stitch by stitch.

Arthur Rimbaud
(1854-1891)

Ah seasons   Ah castles   (*O saisons, ô châteaux*)

Seasons yes   And castles
No soul's without its faults

Those seasons   Those castles

I studied sorcery
the key to joy none should evade

Long may it last each time
the Gallic cock performs

However! I'm not keen now –
it took charge of my life

Its spell stole soul and body,
got rid of all I'd tried

What do my verses say?
It made them flee and steal

The hour it leaves me though
will be the hour I die

Such seasons   Such castles

(And if bad luck beguiles me
disgrace must follow after

It's sad but such contempt
offers the quickest death)

The Flags of May   *(Bannières de mai)*

Reaching the clear-cut linden boughs
a sickly horn-call dies away,
but Mays make light songs flutter round
each currant-bush like strips of silk.
May our blood laugh within our veins.
Consider all those writhing vines.
Sky's lovely as an angel – blue
air and blue stream communicate.
I'm off now. Should a sunbeam wound
me I'll just fall on mossy ground.

To wait in patience or get bored –
too easy. I disdain my pain.
Would some dramatic summer hitch
me on to luck's swift chariot.
Will Nature's plenty make me, less
alone, less pointless, die? Whereas
shepherds in love keep dying through
and (funny that) throughout the world.

Oh let the seasons wear me out.
I yield my self to Nature's care.
I'm thirsty and I'm ravenous
but will She slake and nourish me?
I've no illusions. All's a farce –
what parents do, what the sun does.
But I wish nothing to laugh at.
Will lack of luck unshackle me?

May 1872

Seascape *(Maritime)*

Chariots silver, bronze –
Prows steel, silver –
    batter the foam
    lift thorned stubs

Streams from the moor –
Ruts gouged by backsurge –
    flow curved to the east
    to props of the forest
    to struts for the pier
    angles struck by whirled light

Rainer Maria Rilke
(1875-1926)

Endymion

The hunt's still with him and the quarry breaks
   as through a thicket through his veins.
   Valleys occur and forest pools
reflect the doe pursued by the quick pulse
of that sound sleeper who's bewildered once
   again when bow and arrows blurred
   in dream dissolve so speedily.
The goddess though, young, never wed, the one
   who passes over every night
of time, replenishing herself, alone,
high in the skies, concerned with no-one, came
   down lightly to his languid side
   and as she leaned to look at him
his skin started to glimmer while he slept.

Childhood *(Kindheit)*

There runs the fear of school away, long hours
spent waiting, other stale and silly things.
Such loneliness, such weighty loss of time . . .
And then release: the sparkling streets, the noise
and in the squares the lift of fountains and
in parks you see how wide a world can be
though wearing through it all short trousers so
unlike the others going to and fro . . .
Time so crammed with wonder, passing time,
such loneliness . . .

And in all this to look beyond and far:
men here and women, men, more women there
and children all so different, brightly dressed,
a house then, here and there a dog and times
when silent panic alternates with trust. . .
Such pointless grief, such dreams, such dread,
such depth unending . . .

And then to play with ball and hoop inside
a garden losing colour all the time
and often running into grown-ups in
wild haste not looking where you're going till
you're heading home at dusk obediently
taking stiff tiny steps, grasped by a hand . . .
So many things to learn which drift away,
such burdens, such alarm . . .

And kneeling by the limitless grey pond
for hours on end, clutching a small boat and
forgetting it since all those similar
and finer yachts keep skimming round,
remembering one small and pallid face
sinking like a reflection from the pond . . .
Childhood, comparisons which slide away,
where did they go? Oh where?

People by Night *(Menschen bei Nacht)*

Nights are not meant for crowds or passers-by.
Your neighbour's cut off from you by each night.
Perhaps you shouldn't try to seek him out.
If you illuminate your room by night
planning to look at someone in the eye
you'd better be convinced who it'll be.

Men get distorted strangely by the light.
It ricochets to watchers from their face
so if they get together in the night
they'll see a flinching world that's not quite right.
That yellow glow staining the brow's expelled
clear thought and what's called commonsense.
Liquor keeps flickering vaguely in their glance
and from their hands henceforth only depend
the useless clumsy gestures they must use
attempting to decode each other's words –
but when they start to talk of *I* and *I*
they're designating someone else entirely.

The Mount of Olives *(Der Ölbaum-Garten)*

Climbing the slope beneath grey leaves he just
seemed grey and tousled like the olive-trees.
He hid his burning forehead streaked with dust
in hands as grey and dusty as the trees.

This after all. The end of the affair.
I'm going on while I am going blind
and wondering why You make me say You're there
when You are now impossible to find.

I can no longer find You. You're unknown.
Not in me. Nor in others. Nor this stone.
I can no longer find You. I'm alone.

I'm all alone with all man's pain and grief.
Through You I was supposed to bring relief.
You're nowhere. I'm a charlatan and thief.

We're told an angel came. That's past belief –

And why an angel? Nothing came but night
rustling so casually through the trees.
The disciples stirred. Their dreams incurred disease.
And why an angel? Nothing came but night.

The night that came was not unusual.
Hundreds have come and gone that way.
Dogs kept on sleeping. All the stones stayed still.
One sad night passed like any other till
a normal dawn brought on another day.

Angels don't come to those who pray like me
and nights will give significance to the rest.
All's lost to those who've lost themselves. At best
their fathers will disown them and decree
they're banned from sheltering on their mother's breast.

The Lay of the Love and Death of Cornet Christoph Rilke von Langenau (1899, rev. 1906)

(Die Weise von Liebe und Tod des Cornets Christoph Rilke von Langenau)

"... den 24. November 1663 wurde Otto von Rilke / auf Langenau / Gränitz und Ziegra / zu Linda mit seines in Ungarn gefallenen Bruders Christoph hinterlassenem Anteile am Gute Lina beliehen; doch mußte er einen Revers ausstellen / nach welchem die Lehensreichung null und nichtig sein sollte / im Falle sein Bruder Christoph (der nach beigebrachtem Totenschein als Cornet in der Kompagnie des Freiherrn von Pirovano des kaiserl. österr. Heysterschen Regiments zu Roß ... verstorben war) zurückkehrt ..."

"on the 24th of November 1663 Otto von Rilke auf Langenau came into an inheritance left by his brother Christoph who had been killed in Hungary. However, there is a counter-bill according to which the inheritance is null and void since, according to the death-certificate, his brother Christoph was killed when he was a Cornet [the soldier who bears the regimental flag] in the Company of Baron von Pirovano in the Imperial Austrian Cavalry Regiment ..."

Riding, riding, riding, through the day, through the night, through the day.

Riding, riding, riding.

And courage is so exhausted while longing remains so strong. There are no hills now, hardly even a tree. Nothing risks standing up. Strange huts squat thirstily near a marsh for water. There's not a tower to be seen anywhere. Always the view's the same. We have two eyes, too many. Only at night sometimes can any of us know where we're going. Do we perhaps ride back in the dark to the same bit of land we fought so hard to win under a strange sun? That could be true. The sun's strong here, the way it is at home in the depth of summer. It was summertime when we left. The clothes women wore then shone in green fields. We've been riding for so long. It must be autumn now. At least the women back there know about us and are sad.

Von Langenau turns in his saddle and says "Herr Marquis…" For three days now the slim little Frenchman behind him has never stopped chattering and laughing. Now he doesn't know what to say. He's like a child who'd like to sleep. There's dust on his white lace collar. He doesn't notice this. He'd only like to sink down slowly in his velvet saddle.

But Von Langenau smiles and says "You don't seem to see very well, Herr Marquis. Surely for your mother you'd be looking more like—"

This makes the little Frenchman bloom once more. He shakes the dust from his lace collar and looks brand new and ready for anything.

Each soldier talks about his mother. One of the Germans isn't at all shy about it. He brings his words out slowly, clearly. Like a girl arranging a bouquet, testing flower by flower so thoughtfully, not really knowing what they'll look like as a whole. He's fitting his words together like that. In pleasure? In sorrow? They all keep listening. Even the spitting stops. Because, like him, they enjoy hearing themselves talk. And anyone in the crowd who can't speak German can still catch the odd phrase: "One evening . . ." "When I was little . . ."

They're all near each other now, soldiers coming from France and Burgundy, from the Netherlands, from out of the valleys of Carinthia, from Bohemian castles, from the Emperor Leopold himself. They all know what he's talking about. It's almost as though there's only *one* mother . . .

So they ride away into the evening, into any evening. They say nothing but then they've brought lucid words with them. The Marquis takes off his helmet. His dark hair is soft and, as he lowers his head, it falls on to his neck the way a girl's would. Now von Langenau understands something: a long way away, standing out, a radiance, something slender, something shadowy. A lonely statue, half decayed. And long after, much later, it occurs to him that it was a Madonna.

Watchfire. They all sit down and wait. Wait, hoping someone will sing. But they're all so tired. The reddish light is harsh. It reaches the dusty boots. Creeps to the knees, peers into folded hands. But it doesn't have wings. Faces stay dark. Even so, the eyes of the little Frenchman light up for a moment with a same kind of glow. He's kissed a small rose then put it back to wither against his chest. Von Langenau saw him do that because he can't seem to fall asleep. He thinks: I don't have a rose, not a single one.

Then he begins to sing. And it's an old sad song that girls back at home sing in the fields, in autumn, when the harvest is almost over.

The little Marquis says "You are very young aren't you, sir?" And Von Langenau, half sorrowful half defiant, answers, "Eighteen." Then they fall silent.

Later on the Frenchman asks "Have you got a fiancée?"

"What about yourself?" von Langenau hurls this back at him.

"She's blonde. Like you, Herr Junker."

And they fall silent once again until the German cries out "But then why the devil d'you just sit in a saddle, ride at those Turkish dogs, gallop all over this poisonous bloody land?"

The Marquis smiles. "So as to go back home again."

And von Langenau's face goes sad. He thinks about the blonde girl he used to play with. Wild games. And he'd like to go home, just for a moment, just long enough to say "Magdalena – I know I was always like that. Forgive me."

"*Like* . . . *was?* thinks the young Junker. – And they're far away from each other.

One day, during the morning, a man on horseback turns up, then another, then four more, ten. All of them big and tall. In armour. And then a thousand coming up behind: the army.

They'll have to part.

"Go home safely, Herr Marquis –"

"May Our Lady protect you, Herr Junker."

And they can't leave each other. They're friends for life, brothers. They've trusted one another, learnt so much about each other. Hesitate. All around them there's a hurrying and clatter of hooves. The Marquis slips his right glove off. Brings the tiny rose out, chooses a petal for him. The way a priest would place a wafer on the palm.

"It'll look after you. Farewell. For now."

Von Langenau doesn't know what to do. He looks longingly at the Frenchman, then puts this foreign petal inside his greatcoat where it will drift up and down on the tides of his heart. A horn is blown. The Junker rides up to his regiment and smiles sadly. He is protected by a woman he's never met.

One day all the camp-followers turn up. Cursing, colours, laughter. They dazzle the countryside. Lively boys running around. Scuffling. Yelling. Harlots arrive with purple hats on their floating hair. Becks and calls. Mercenaries come wearing iron, black like wandering nightfall. They grab the whores violently, rip their clothes, push them where the drums are kept. And from the eager hands of soldiers the drums awake, rumble as if inside a dream, go on rumbling. – And in the twilight lanterns get held out. Makeshift ones, odd-looking. And wine, glinting on the helmets. Wine? Or blood? – Who can tell the difference?

Before Count Spork at last. He's standing by his white horse, towering. His long hair's the colour of iron.

Von Langenau hasn't had to ask. He knows the General and leaps from his steed to give a salute out of a cloud of dust. He brings a message commending himself but the Count merely gives an order "Read me what's on that scrap of paper."

His lips didn't move. They don't need to. They're good enough to curse with. For anything further he just gestures with his right hand. That's it. Anybody'll see what he means. The young man hasn't quite got to the end. He's unsure where he stands. The General's in front of them all. Even the sky's not there. Then Spork, the great general, speaks:

"Carry the flag, Cornet."

That's all. Quite enough.

The Company lies beyond the River Raab. Von Langenau rides away, alone. Over a flat piece of land. In twilight. Metalwork on the saddle glints through the dust. And then the moon rises. He sees the shine on his hands.

He has a dream.
But someone screams out to him.
Screams, screams,
tears his dream apart.
That's no owl. It's a yell for help:
the only tree there is
calls out:
"You there!"
And he sees a shape leaning against it,
a woman, bleeding, naked.
He hears what she's saying:
"Get me free!"

And he springs into the green darkness,
cuts through the cords
sees her eyes glowing
her teeth grinding.

Is she laughing?

He's afraid,
gets on his horse,

gallops into the night,
the cords gripped in his fist are wet with blood.

Von Langenau's writing a letter in gratitude. He makes the letters large, upright, serious.

> *"My dear Mother,*
> *"Be proud: I carry the flag,*
> *"Don't worry: I carry the flag,*
> *"Love me: I carry the flag —"*

Then he sticks the letter inside his greatcoat, on a secret place. Near the rose-petal. And he thinks: it'll soon smell sweet. And the thinks: maybe someone else will find it . . . And he thinks again . . . Because the enemy is close.

They are riding over a slain farmer. His eyes stay wide open and something is mirrored in them but not the sky. Later they hear dogs howling. There's a village. At last. And above the huts a castle like a rocky hill. They come up to the drawbridge. There's a huge gate. A welcome blow on a horn. Listen: rumbling, rattling, hounds barking. Neighing in the courtyard, horses kicking, summons.

Repose! To be a guest for once. Not just to get for yourself what you can afford. Not always having to grab things frenziedly. Just for once letting it all come and know that what you're getting is bound to be good. Forget about bravery for a while and tumble between silk sheets. Not always just being a soldier. Letting your hair go loose for once, sprawling in an easy chair with a white collar on, feeling all's well all over, right to the fingertips. After a bath. To learn again what women look like. How they cope with colour like whites and blues; what hands they have and how they sing and laugh when blond boys bring beautiful dishes in, laden with juicy fruits.

It started over dinner. Turned into a festival, no-one really understood why. Torches flaring, voices bawling, weird songs clinking from glass and glitter and then, as soon as all's fallen in rhythm: dance. Everyone swept away like waves breaking in the solar – losing each other and finding each other – glare of enjoyment and light that's blinding – swaying of summer winds into the clothes of woman so warm.

From the darkness of wine and a thousand roses the hour runs rustling into the dream of nightfall.

There's one who stands and stares into this splendour. And he's so well-disposed that he waits to make sure he's awake. Because only in sleep can anyone observe such finery, such a celebration with women like that: their slightest gesture makes a pleat recurring in brocade. They create hours from silver conversations and often lift their hands somehow – and you have to fancy they go somewhere you don't know to fold soft roses you'll never see. And then you dream – to be decked out like them, pleased in a different way and to deserve a crown for your vacant forehead.

One who is wearing white silk knows he can't wake up because he is awake and bewildered far from reality. So

he flees scared into the dream to stand unmoving in the park, alone in the black park. And he asks a woman who is nodding her head at him.
"Are you the night?"
She smiles.
He feels ashamed about his white clothes.
And wants to be far off and alone and armed.
Well-armed.

Have you forgotten you are my page for to-day? Why have you abandoned me? Where are you off to? Your clothes tell me you're –"

"Do you wish you were wearing your ordinary coat?"

"Are you cold? – Are you perhaps homesick?"
The Countess smiles.
No. That's only because childhood, that soft dark cloak, has fallen from his shoulders. Who has taken it off? "You?" he asks in a voice he's never heard before. "You!"
And now there's nothing on him. He's naked like a penitent. Luminous and slender.

The castle loses its light slowly. A heaviness now: being weary or in love or drunk. After so many long empty nights in the open beds. Wide, oak beds. Where you don't say your prayers as you did on your way here, lying in a damp furrow like a grave, trying to fall asleep.
"Lord God. As Thou wilt."
Prayers are shorter in bed.
More heartfelt though.

The tower chamber is dark.
But they lighten faces by smiling. They fumble on their way as if they are blind and discover each other like a doorway. Almost like children who, frightened by the night, keep close to each other. And yet they aren't afraid. Nothing is against them – neither yesterday, nor to-morrow; because time has collapsed. And they are emerging like blossom from the rubble.

He does not ask, "Your husband?"

She does not ask, "Your name?"

They've found one another so they can put on a new identity.

They'll give each other a hundred new names and then take them away again, lightly, the way you'd lift off an earring.

In the entrance-hall some armour, a shoulder-belt and the greatcoat belonging to von Langenau are hanging over a chair. His gloves are lying on the floor. His flag, dark and long, droops on its staff leaning against the crossbars of a window. Outside, a storm races across the sky, breaking the night into pieces, white pieces, black ones. The moonlight skims past like a drawn-out lightning flash and the flag which doesn't move has restless shadows. It is dreaming.

Was a window open? Has the storm got inside the castle? Who's slamming those doors? Who's just passing through the room? –

Leave him alone. Doesn't matter who it is. He won't find anything in the tower chamber. Behind a hundred doors lies an ample sleep that two have in common – like *one* mother or *one* death.

Can it be morning? What's that sunrise? It's very big. Is that noise birds? You can hear them all over the place?
Everything's bright but it isn't daybreak.
Everything's loud but it's not birds we're hearing.
It's the rafters. They're burning. It's the windows that are screaming. Everyone's screaming, scarlet in the face, screaming to the enemy standing outside in the flickering landscape, screaming: *Fire.*

And with sleep torn from them they all force their way, half of them in iron, half of them wearing nothing, rushing from room to room, rushing all over the place, trying to find the staircase.

And horns with forced breath stammer in the courtyard.
Gather round! Gather round!
Quivering drums.

But the flag is not there.
Shouts: Cornet!
Maddened horses, prayers, screaming,
Curses: *Cornet!*
Iron clashing iron, commands, signals.
Silence. Then: CORNET!
And again: *CORNET!*
And away with the thundering cavalry.

But the flag is not with them.

Running now as fast as possible he's pushing through doors on fire, gets scorched descending the stairs, breaks out of the raging castle with the flag on his arms as if he was holding a pale unconscious woman. He finds a horse like a scream with hoofs and gallops ahead, past everything once gone by, to be again with his own people. The flag's coming where it belongs, it's never looked so regal and now they all recognise far in the distance a shining man with no helmet who's bearing the flag . . .

But it starts to gleam, twists about, turns larger, goes red.

Their flag is burning in the midst of the enemy and they're rushing towards it.

Von Langenau is in the thick of the enemy but not alone. Terror has formed a circle around him and he checks his steed in the centre under his slowly blazing flag.

He looks around slowly, almost wistfully. So much that is strange, so many bright colours in front of him. Gardens – he thinks for a moment then smiles. But he feels that eyes are holding him, recognises men and knows who they are, heathen dogs – and he urges his horse among them.

But when the horse got knocked down under him he found gardens again, also the sixteen curved sabres leaping at him, catching the light, ray by ray, like a fête.

A laughing fountain.

The greatcoat caught fire in the castle, along with the letter and the rose-petal that once belonged to a woman from a foreign land.

Next spring (it came sadly and cold) a messenger from the Baron of Pirovano rode slowly into Langenau. He has seen an old woman weeping there.

Marie Luise Kaschnitz
(1901-1974)

Spirals

We put down words on cowhide
who'd bother to read anything
that wasn't written on cowhide?
Five dollars for anyone who still understands our language
and will pay attention to a poem.
The rain listens
so does the indifferent sunset
that's not enough.
The dog's coat bristles
he shivers and howls near the ford
that's not enough.
The dreamer tumbles from the roof
he went spiralling down
whorled ammonite for a gravestone
that's enough.

Unsaid

Unsaid
whatever there was to say about the sun
and the truth about lightning
not to speak of love.

Attempts. Petitions. Failed.
An inadequate description.

Daybreak let go of
No mention of the sower
And nothing noticed by the path except
one buttercup and a violet

Your backbone unbraced
by eternal salvation
Decay not gainsaid
nor despair

Satan not pushed to the wall
since I don't believe in him
God not praised
but then who am I that

Rolf Haufs
(1935–)

Peppino Portiere

When he discovered leaves
he'd sweep them off the gravel
with a straw broom.

He had a cap.
He had a satchel.
He had a bicycle.

Towards midday he'd order
some sunlight so he could
sit in the shadow.

He gave advice.
He spoke to his chickens.
He phoned all over the world.

He took a eucalyptus on
when there was a contest
about age and wisdom.

The tree won.

Rolf-Dieter Brinkmann
(1942-1975)

Self-Portrait in the Supermarket
for Dieter Wellershoff

In the super-
market's big window

I come across myself
as I really am

The shock's not
the one I expected
but all the same
it gives me quite
a turn. And I move on
till I'm standing in front
of a bare wall and know
nothing further.

Someone'll
surely
come and pick me up there

later on.

Even More Shadows

We're sitting beneath a big
tree in summer and can't account
for it. When the afternoon's

here, the shape of this shadow
alters and the pills
you keep swallowing don't

help you make out more clearly
the man in the distance
who's following a definite

track with his dog. Still more
shadows find their place in the shadow
thrown by this tree down

the slope while we go on
sitting here hoping
the waitress will bring us

coffee. She's still standing
in front of the mirror wiping
her mouth with toilet paper.

Then she approaches me
smiling but you don't notice.
The lipstick she's been using

is the only thing in the world
which helps us identify
the outline of her figure in the shadow

because now the tree is stirring
all its leaves without
altering its standpoint.

Each single leaf casts a bigger
Shadow. But you don't know that.

Jean Cassou
(1897-1986)

Jean Cassou was arrested on 13 December 1941 and kept in solitary confinement with no books or writing materials. Knowing that he would be executed if he were found guilty of treason he nonetheless composed in his head 33 amazing sonnets. Tried in 1942 and found not guilty he was transferred to a harsh prison-camp until 1943, when he was able to send his sonnets under the name of "Jean Noir" to the poet Louis Aragon, who ran a clandestine publishing centre in Monaco under the pseudonym François La Colère. Aragon coined this lovely image in admiration of Cassou's tenacity: "He had to save each poem as if he were holding a child's head above water".

Cassou, seriously wounded on the eve of Liberation, left the Communist Party in 1945 to be vilified by many friends before being appointed Director of the new Museum of Modern Art. He was awarded the Légion d'honneur in 1982 and the Grand Prix de la Société des gens de lettres the following year. He died in 1986.

Timothy Adès has splendidly translated these cryptic and elusive poems, which were published by Arc in 2004. Readers might be interested in comparing these two radically different attempts to bring these 33 sonnets into English. Adès scrupulously manages to match the original in every conceivable way, never at a loss to find the necessary word or rhyme. My own approach is more to interpret than echo, an attempt to discover the inner meaning of poems which deserve the same kind of co-operative attentiveness required by Maurice Scève's *Délie*, the esoteric *Chimères* of Nerval or Mallarmé's later sonnets, all of which I had studied at the Sorbonne in 1954-5 while wrestling with my thesis *La Conception du néant chez Mallarmé* for the Diplôme d'études supérieures ("mention Assez bien"!).

In 2008 philip kuhn's itinerant press brought out a most beautiful limited edition of these translations under the two titles *Composés au secret* and *From a Condemned Cell*. The 33 booklets published were hand-bound. Tucked furtively into the back cover for readers to find, as if time and place were still 1944 in Monaco, were the complete texts of the poems in French by "Jean Noir" and "présentés par François La Colère". Each one cost an appropriate £33. The binding was a cold white with deliberately faint blue lettering and the booklet delicately small enough to be kept in a pocket in case there were suspicious eyes around.

33 Sonnets

I

Long as a dream among the stars, the ship
of death glides with no sail. One passenger
flat on his back, eyes staring far from sleep,
drifts like a flower on water who knows where.

Shall I risk trying the royal game to-night,
turn back inside my arms the murmuring stream
then, outlined in a pale shroud, sit up straight
like some tall tower crumbling near a tomb?

Darkness already quails when I pass by.
The corpse inside me shivers in its chains
as though my real name was Nobody.

A silent cry like a dog's phantom runs
life-givingly across me from my brow
as compass to my feet that form the prow.

II

Dead to all fortune, promise, room for breath –
though not to time avid for harvesting –
I must redeem myself, give up my berth
and stripped of hope face increased suffering.

I take pain with me to a nameless land
where night pressing on night effaces me.
Shadows eat shadows. I walk brazenly
though dream-walls muffle tracks I leave behind.

Not life. Not void. The stillborn children from
my vigils wander in the interim.
Transparent clarities which come and go –

spurts with no future – memories with no past:
their joy is failure and their sport is woe
while Psyche's wings outspread burn in their breast.

III

I've missed my way by snow-capped peaks my skull
hides in the night-time of its maze. I feel
I've no choice left as an itinerant
trapped in the crypt bricked up by my lament.

Stray in this labyrinth and then go mad!
Oh sacred dreams of my imprisonment –
gaols are my private captives, made, unmade,
as deeper mirrors mimic my complaint.

I'm lost so high no-one can listen to
my smothered plea like one last streak of blue.
Down in that clear land where the dawns begin

my shepherdess will surely understand.
Should someone whisper "It's your father" then
come to these heights and take me by the hand.

IV

I had a dream I bore you in my arms
up from the courtyard to your darkened chamber.
You seemed exactly like each girl whose charms
draw me – but had we met? I can't remember.

The night was moonlit, frostbound – just the night
to move through echoes of some enterprise.
You shivered in the cold and felt so light.
I tried without success to see your eyes.

I lost you like so many things a dream
or worldly matters offered to my heart –
pearls guarding secrets, rose without a stain.

Signposts of memory, enigmas, I'm
counselled by every hard-won dawn to greet
with open eyes each masterpiece of pain.

V

There will be poets back on earth some day
who'll see the lake and the enchanted cave,
the groves of Arcady where children play,
the Vale of Promises, moments of love

lost now to memory, girls they didn't know
who wept, the House of Sin, joys which delude
so magically and times when they felt proud
to have a kiss placed on their lonely brow.

They'll recognise, behind masks worn by some
crazed women dancing in a carnival,
their finest poem freed at last from all

the sobs that gave them birth. Then, satisfied
they'll go home in the twilight blessing fame,
love everlasting, waves and wind and blood.

VI

Far sounds of life guessed at from secrecy
as horns blare, children yell let out from school,
church-bells announce to-morrow's festival,
a car heads blindly for eternity –

all stifled by the mute walls of a gaol.
What guardian-spirits (ill-luck or the night)
can guide me to the canyon of your street?
I grope in thought to touch you, sense your smile.

To merit meeting those deep mysteries
I've rid myself of every sort of light.
Light straightaway gets clustered in your cries.

I want to pass back through the iron gate
carrying in me these dark ricochets –
stars from my cell, flowers on inverted skies.

VII

Drink from this cup of darkness then you'll sleep.
We'll pick your plight up like a funeral-wreath
and take it to those gardens pledged to death.
You'll shiver like a sleepwalker and slip

out through the door no-one can use to pluck
the myrtle with gold branches and the red
anemone whose brilliance will make
the night around you young again and lead

you to the frontiers of true life and pure
achievement. There, all dreams have certainty,
terror and power. You'll recognise them all

in the blue dawn of a perpetual
to-morrow. Healed at last, you'll wake up where
three Muses wait: Love, Freedom, Poetry.

VIII

There were just lacerated trees with rooks
    above them flapping clumsily
    on that iron evening when I
came to that château colourless as frost.

I had brought nothing with me – neither books
    nor sin-infected soul (my best
    companion) nor that girl-child
who'd dreamed of living in the outside world.

Milk from the Sphinx had made the walls turn white.
    Flagstones looked red with Orpheus' blood.
Indifferent hands had hung the washing out

from windows leary as a fairy's glance.
    The stage was set for actors who'd
gone crazed and cruel from too much radiance.

IX

(*Translated from Hugo von Hofmannsthal*)

She held the cup up near her face
with such a sure and steady hand
and walked with such an even pace
no drop got spilt upon the ground.

He sat upon a restive horse.
Displaying sureness in control
he tugged the reins with such mild force
the steed immediately stood still.

However, when one gentle hand
offered the one still gloved in steel
the little cup she'd brought, she found

they were both trembling now so much
that when their hands began to touch
drops of black wine were made to spill.

X

That song we heard . . . Remember how the night
got scratched and starred with rockets bursting high
above the beach? We marvelled at the sight
like children at their first festivity.

Naïvely joyous on our balcony
we looked down at the dancers in the street.
And yet, my love, your gaze seemed shadowy.
Turning that page in fear we tempted fate.

That summer, suddenly, we felt the claw
of maddened hope catch on our skin. That goad
is lodged perhaps forever in our side

for, all along our lives, we know for sure
a beast whose hunger's never satisfied
prowls in the forest, sensing where we tread.

XI

My guiding star has only let you see
a dark face, a set mouth and empty eyes –
signs, dear one, of so much aridity.
Nothing but shadow forms my chief disguise.

For whom then were my glances and the pure
music which trickled through my fingers when
time seemed so clear? My Asian pledges soon
flowed to the dead end of the hemisphere.

Go back now to your light. Lean over your
reflection like Narcissus freed from pride,
desire and grief – perplexed and blushing at

your beauty which increases year by year.
You alone license me to immolate
happiness formed by everything I dread.

XII

Dreams hard at work, clutching each other's hand,
make one black path of all the lengths I've run
whispering what I'm loath to understand.
With you, because you've known what's going on,

I just see figments, pain and penalties,
tired stars above friends out at exercise,
while, lacking mirrors, straggling discords find
no resonance nor logic for their sound.

There's comfort in comparing our two skies –
like yours, though, mine's filled to the brim with gall.
My vision's dazzled by our common plight

and gapes with flame as all around eyes blaze –
blue galaxies studding a peacock's tail –
your gaze shipwrecked on dark reefs of my night.

XIII

The street ascends to a blue laundry, bare
until it carves a notch in the chalk sky.
You, veteran of bruised paving-stones, pass by
dusty stalls, benches shivering on the square.

All you watch turns to stone – posters with their
fixed scream, shattered boutiques with every shard
of glass immobilised and each façade
as houses wait for the squad to open fire!

Get on your way. Leave our roads as they were.
You couldn't ever find a destiny!
The echo of your footsteps makes this silence.

Our roofs and window-panes must one day cry
out laughing. Those royal gardens which your presence
weighs down with ash will then burst into flower!

XIV

Like covert meanings in some childish song
we've dreamed of one day hearing our own voice,
meeting our glance and following the trace
left by our footfalls as we walk along.

Our love's been faulty. Time, wanted for fraud,
filched our time from us then fled with a sneer,
leaving a shred of that sly tune he'd played
to soothe us both. At moments it's seemed clear

this life does not belong to us. But that
is wrong. It's no-one else's. It's still ours.
That vagrant girl with broken hands who sat

one stormy evening by our cold fireside –
look at her now, beware the way she stares:
two sickly stars, the eyes of some sad bird.

XV

When the two of us approach that Chinese town
I shall limp a bit but know the facts of love.
Crazy paupers hunched beneath some ox-carts down
by the fevered walls with gated towers above

will take wing to guide us to the reservoirs
as a moon, lukewarm to match the setting sun,
greets us with a file of lanterns while our ears
catch low cries those clashing cymbals cannot drown.

I'll walk clinging to your robe and, as before,
just rely on kisses hinted by your glance –
eyes that promise bliss and music and soft prayers.

That will be an unexpected recompense –
to discover, like the glint from two lost stars
now rekindled, breath in our frail souls once more.

XVI

Admoto occurrere fato.
           (Lucan, IV 480)

We'll find him where the road turns off to grief,
level with night and easy to see through.
Till now, his replica was all we knew.
At last he's slinking closer like a thief.

We've been two effigies of silence, mere
shadows unkeen to link fake hands. Yet both
our hands, gloved suddenly again with truth,
will bless the dreaded envoy edging near.

It's getting darker and it's late. Why must
this life in death drag on relentlessly?
If there's a thread of twilight left now – just

one ring of blood around that bitter cup
held back by a grinning angel from our lip –
let's kill the angel then we'll drink the sea.

XVII

Go right away. Don't make a noise. Just get
on board. Set sail and never come back here.
Straight home each one of you – and don't forget
your alien shadows, lutes and false lodestar.

Of course for such proud walkers all this made
one novel venture tinged with sorcery.
Get rid of it like stolen jewellery,
a flame still flickering, a book you've read.

This is the room where angels come to die.
Leave us alone in our forgotten life.
Our wings hang useless, our hands droop unmanned.

Since dawn we've lived a terrifying lie
both curious and tender past belief –
a tale only despair can understand.

XVIII

Those stars who chose their victim with shrill cries
of warning and continue their pursuit
may quench their anger should he stray about
the fiery world, unseen by any eyes,

a sorry ghost, a shadow out of reach –
like Rilke's Prodigal Son whom custom drove
to flee to distance from a home where each
remembrance loved him with oppressive love.

Friends blurred in night, concerned for him, don't need
to pray for news or seek him any more.
And may the dead, burdened with pardoning,

hover no longer near his lonely shore –
for he's that stag in tears with lowered head
who'll find them in his dreams each evening.

XIX

Je suis Jean.
        (Victor Hugo)

I'm John. I bring no message. I saw less
than nothing in my island-gaol and thought
of nothing to cry in the wilderness.
I simply nursed a dream one summer night.

I dreamed of youth regained beneath the blaze
of stars lighting another age than ours
because I long to decode languages
seared on the night-sky by these meteor showers.

My rôle is to stay silent and to wait.
I don't feel up to weaving auguries
aspiring to the dawn. No hymns console

my brow though they disclose bright mysteries.
Disciple, forerunner, lost in the night,
sleepless, white shadows mirroring the whole!

XX

For house of fire now read stone sky,
but for stone sky read angel's wing
that rustles with an iron reply.
By light which alterations bring

you are the merest stir of air –
a fragile language which may veer
the cutting wind of adverse times
and set up alien regimes.

Let living daybreak turn to brass,
rock to the fog of destiny:
let poker-faced insiders jeer

urged on by prouder treachery.
Snow now. Does Christmas in its lair
concoct a steel antithesis?

XXI

i.m. Antonio Machado

Dear honoured soul, may Charity
guiding saints through the darkened hours
alight on these dishonoured shores
your torch-flame cannot purify.

They'll save your ashes from a land
so arid it resembles sand
and scatter them like bright birds where
skies still hold hope of purer air.

There'll you retrieve scents which retain
your deeper summers spent in tears.
Here only fragments will remain

from one smashed urn in anger thrown
against a gaol where prisoners
lie rotting behind walls of stone.

XXII

In every country since the start of time
workers have died. Their pools of blood still stain
our streets. Coughing in smoke they fall and scream
till slain by hunger, cold, fire, wheels of iron.

In every country where the stones are raw,
trees rotten, bars on windows red with rust –
day in day out where poverty's the law
they're led like beasts to slaughter on sawdust.

O God of Justice, reigning not above
but hidden in the raging heart of man,
re-form the world by judgement winged with love.

Lord of the strong, open your eyes and scan
the plight of workers on the earth – their tongue
is clamped, their wrists are bound, their chain is long.

XXIII

Since the month cherries ripened on the trees
a wound inside my heart oozes each day.
Vainly the lilacs sunlit in the breeze
caress suburban walls in makeshift play.

The country of blue rooftops and grey songs –
bleeding nonstop despite the love it wears –
can't provide reasons why my pulse still longs
for those old courtyards rusty with our tears.

I tell the elves I meet along the way
how Hugo's novel deals with suffering.
The tree in the school playground too explains:

Oh yes, things will improve. But when? . . . Some day . . .
To make sure next year has a proper spring
let's use our fists and knock away the guns.

XXIV

Briques et tuiles, etc.
       (Verlaine)

Iron, lead and zinc:
cramped hells remove
all thoughts of love –
what did you think?

Desert and sea:
no new events
make any sense
that I can see.

Each time we play
Zero contrives
mate in three moves.

Cancel endeavour
since history may
close down for ever.

XXV

I saw Paris again, her statues draped
in blood, her sky grey as an aircraft's wing.
Sunset. Someone far off began to sing
as though somewhere a plume of sparks upleaped.

I loved that town so long – so long ago.
One room had honeyed walls as luminous
as ancient dawns. The ceilings slanted low.
A mirror held a calm face in its ice.

The furniture was all mahogany.
Flute on a marble shelf. A leaded pane
showed chestnuts flaunting leaves almost too green.

I know. I stood once near that window while
the pavements echoed with some festival –
an everyday occurrence like the sea.

XXVI

Once I've evoked each feature I adore,
    presences from the past,
all those gleaned harmonies preserve far more
    than what's supposed to last.

Oh, my fair loves, your gilded lands reflect
    that painted image where
already those farewells which disconnect
    stay equal to your pure

eternities. Our strangled voices – bold
for once – will go on praising all you claim
    never to cease. I'll see

even my own heart shattered willingly.
The most deprived of men dies overcome
    through having loved the world.

XXVII

Your night's less black than usual because,
dear friend, to honour you they've gone ahead
and lit the lamps to make your château blaze.
Their gleam's already stealing towards your bed.

An alien realm of conquest and display,
hunched in the dusk prepared to spring, constrained
you to perfect your curtained shadows stained
ingeniously with ink to shut out day.

A glass of dark milk shot with glints of sun –
all offerings to death revert to light.
Flowers holding secrets die as lightning-fruit.

Favoured with winter visits you well know
how sea-gates open where the walls of iron
are hardest the way skin-wounds start to flow.

XXVIII

One pleasure nourishes these hours I spend alone –
telling my heart I know what used to be. And then
I place my certainty in jumbled narratives
peopling a polar continent with fictive lives.

I keep remembering one evening when a lute
left on a table in some inn sounded a note
that matched a dream about to form. And I've beheld
a wayfarer who dragged his secret round the world.

After so many risks, captives near death can hear,
like a farewell, some song sung by a fisherman
off in the sunlight of the gulf. And there have been

brief, cherished moments spared for fantasy, most dear
of friends. Life's slammed the door once more on couples who're
in love. A hand has passed across each hemisphere.

XXIX

Wardrobe-mistress to the dead, form a princess
out of that corpse bare as a wave-smoothed stone.
Work with your hands the most involved caress
which ever thrilled her to the marrow-bone.

Let night trace bluer shadows in her hair,
a fiery moon uncover her closed eyes.
Shed on her breasts a glaze of snow. She'll wear
on naked arms such radiant fripperies.

I'll see her from now on enthroned in space
lifting a flower up level with her face
or tramping like a sentry up and down

the ramparts, proud and eager to waylay
a fascinated band of lookers-on
though, like a snake in silk, out to betray.

XXX

Gold skeleton stretched out by a sealed wall,
the sleeper, open-eyed, flaunts victory
from misery and that dazzled treasure full
of schemes so tolerant when dreams betray.

As for those stubborn pools in graveyards, throats
of nightingales, each artisan who sweats,
ropes coiled at daybreak, hammers, flour-mills,
cries, blossom, coffins, cog- or prayer-wheels . . .

Each scribe's as joyful as the pen he plies –
surveyors – painters – each exacting hand –
the eye that sums things up – splendour of days

equalling splendour chronicled by nights.
Dear strollers-by, so carefree, pluck our fruits!
Steal ripe grapes and love-apples from our land!

XXXI

Under the blurred grid of this gallery
should one bruised lyre, darkened with anguish, dare
one plucked sound in a lightning-flash we'd see
the radiant athlete of the future there.

Sword brandished on the steps where monsters drowse!
Herald of long dawns, bred in filth, you'll be
our champion to hack the vertebrae
of that imposter clinging like disease

to bodies lugged through every wakeful night
who'll never long again for a dead sleep.
Eyes will not wish to doze. Noon with no qualms

will rip the shadows from each envoy's feet.
May this be the last vigil what we keep.
If we must dream, let's dream the death of dreams.

XXXII

The cosmos can avenge insults endured –
days grow once more in light – evenings, serene,
let dew fall formed from guiltlessness and blood
surrendering to the night like hands washed clean.

Revenge dropped from above, ruthless, complete!
Forests revive after a thunderstorm.
Though all you'll gain will be a certain calm
once what has been condemned leaves one blank sheet.

That silence, white on wild snow-mantled wings,
by yielding one frenetic cry will gauge
        the true extent of armistice.

Once scorn has smashed all barriers and wrings
the heart about to break, rein in your rage
        and scorning scorn labour for peace.

XXXIII

"Your name?" "Fidelity." "Where are you going?" "I
come from you and go back to you." "Lift that shroud from
your face and let me know if you can possibly
look like that other whom I met once in a dream."

"It's not yet the right time." "I see. So I have no
power over you?" "Hush now. I am, I must confess,
your captive. Every blow from fate you undergo
adds one more touch to my elusive loveliness.

In this true face once it's perfected you will see –
out in the open with your own sky overhead –
each choice of yours accomplished and each wound relieved.

Brief are your loves. All told and all already dead.
But they are still your loves. As for your death, you'll be
taking it with you. Just be steadfast. You'll be saved."

Notes

I   The first sonnet Cassou composed in his cell. Interviewed by Daniel Leuvers in 1973 he described it as having "a definite Egyptian colouration". Lying in the dark he felt like "Osiris on his boat", like "an Egyptian mummy". The "murmuring stream" represents the Nile. The "dog" evokes Anubis who, having helped Isis to inter Osiris, became the guide to the dead.

III   The poetic imagination brings a sort of triumph in the second quatrain as Cassou dares to place the idea of prisons *inside* his mind. There, images come and go like reflections of reality.
    The shepherdess is his daughter Anne-Isabelle.

VII   The myrtle was sacred to Venus. Aeneas plucked a golden bough from an enchanted tree to visit another world in safety. Anemone was the daughter of the wind. The symbolism may be that the poet, escaping from prison in a dream, could rediscover love and be "as free as air" to write his poems down.

VIII   The poet arrived at the military prison in the depth of winter on 13 December 1941.
    As the original is cast in decasyllables, my version uses six shorter lines. Cassou adopted the unusual rhyme-scheme *abba baba* for the two quatrains of Sonnet XI so I hope this justifies the even more orthodox pattern *abbc acdd* in this translation.

IX   Cassou appended a note to this sonnet: "Prisoners were not allowed any reading-matter. One day, however, I happened to find a fragment torn from the German-language newspaper the *Pariser Zeitung*. My cellmate and I devoured each word of that infamous rag. It was after all something to read. With pleasure I discovered in it Hofmannsthal's sonnet *Die Beiden*, a well-known anthology piece which had always charmed me so I endeavoured to turn it into French in the course of one sleepless night."

X   This recalls a festival Cassou and his wife witnessed on holiday in an Andalusian village.

XII   In this sonnet and in no. XVII Cassou seems to be addressing the enemy directly. He uses the familiar *tu* in the intimacy of insult as he hopes for a liberated France one day in the future.

XV This is cast in thirteen-syllable lines – i.e. alexandrines with one extra syllable – so it seemed appropriate to start each line of these pentameters with a stressed syllable.

XVI Shortly before he was temporarily released Cassou was allowed a book or two. He requested the Garnier anthology of Latin poets. The epigraph is taken from Lucan's *Pharsalia*, an unfinished epic taking its name from the Greek plain, site of the Civil War battle when Julius Caesar defeated Pompey on 12 May 48 B.C.

The whole quotation in Loeb's Classical Library runs: "No life is short that gives a man time to slay himself; nor does it lessen the glory of suicide to meet doom at close quarters." The fact Lucan was born in Spain may have lent Cassou a fellow-feeling – also that he committed suicide at the age of 25 in 65 A.D. since for Cassou taking his own life could be an escape from further torment.

XVII Nazism was host to all kinds of unclean superstitions – and, of course, Germany's musical heritage is unforgettable. He tells the enemy to take musical instruments away as they contaminate the French landscape. Also their *fées*, the way they tinkered with black magic and believed crazily the Reich would last a thousand years.

XIX The first line of Hugo's poem in *Les Contemplations* "Ecoutez. Je suis Jean. J'ai vu des choses sombres" refers to Chapter XXII of Revelations. Although "exiled" like St. John the Divine on Patmos, Cassou does not resemble him, nor St. John the Baptist "crying in the wilderness" as the forerunner who bears witness, nor St. John the Belovèd Disciple.

XX In his December gaol Cassou may have been ironically wondering whether some extraordinary twist of fate could mean an unexpected Christmas present like an Allied victory.

XXI The poet Antonio Machado, born in Seville in 1875, fled from Franco's Spain only to die on 22 February 1939 at Collioure, some 90 miles from Cassou's prison in Toulouse.

XXIII *Le Temps des cerises* is a song by J.-B. Clément. During the popular uprising in 1871 known as the *Commune* it became a rallying cry for justice.

Cassou refers to the anguish of characters in Hugo's novel *Les Misérables*.

XXIV   The epigraph comes from *Walcourt*, the first poem in the section *Paysages belges* of Verlaine's 1874 collection *Romance sans paroles*. In July 1872 he and Rimbaud walked from the Franco-Belgian border to Brussels passing through Walcourt, a joyous trek for the two lovers. Cassou, separated from his wife, contrasts his metallic prison with the cosy redbrick inns roofed with tiles which Verlaine refers to as "les charmants / Petits asiles / Pour les amants". Here the sand of the desert and the salt of the sea replace Belgium's hops and vines. The two poets were going somewhere. In the closed and claustrophobic narrative of his cell Cassou cannot but feel checkmate is near.

XXVII   The friend mentioned is Joë Bousquet who, shot in the spine during World War One, had to live virtually housebound. The ink may refer to Bousquet's writings as a protection against the horrors of the Nazi-infested world outside his "curtained shadows".

XXX   In rapture, like Manley Hopkins in *Pied Beauty*, Cassou lists implements and those who wield them, celebrating a world of activity and creativity from which he is separated and realising ruefully that those outside, involved in "normal life", probably take their freedom for granted.

XXXI   "The radiant athlete of the future" is presumably the triumphant effort which will get rid of the invaders, ultimately lulled by the apparent docility of those who would resist. Prisoners lying awake dream of being able to sleep soundly but the poet warns them and himself that they must never sink in the future to a complacent slumber. Eternal vigilance is essential.

XXXII   The "revenge dropped from above" may refer to Allied bombing raids on Occupied France. Cassou realises innocent blood will be spilt and, looking forward to a world he may never see, implores his eventually liberated countrymen to put contempt behind them.

Anne Mounic

the duel now more one-sided than before
(à armes un peu plus inégales qu'auparavent)
> to Claude Vigée, for song drawn from the deepest well
> in spite of everything

I hear that cry of deep distress from one
who's lost his way led far from family,
far from the plinths of tenderness, those bonds
forged from long years with those one's learned to love.
Forsaking stays within, life's power flees,
escapes stabs of awareness – torn
up by the roots (no question there) – and then
there's all that muffled intertwining since
the sap, the fibres rise up to the fore
through agony, disintegrating soon.

I've such respect for one who can
in panic still take on, despite
all else, what's always seemed to be
an angel-conflict all the crueller since
the duel's now more one-sided than before.

Life really is "a bloody-awful mess" –
        that's what he said.

arresting sleights of hand
(de saisissantes transformations)

Sun waking on the snow
foreshadows vanishing the way it prints
forgotten shapes in leisure on the land.
Such changes are alive, go radiant,
can't hinder, given time's transcendence,
erosions or those sudden rifts in earth.
That smooth stream's rising slightly: rivers
can also try arresting sleights of hand.
Each tree now, mimicking an island
traces its silhouette on water.
The world, called suddenly to wakefulness,
mirrors its own awareness as all four
elements resume their primal collusion
inside a universe preferring to
reflect itself rather than disappear.

infinity, conceivable florescence
(son infini, sa floraison possible)

Plenitude, integrity, some inner stirring –
the soul, once one gives in to self from self,
achieves its own new music, depicting
slow flow of river between fields and woods
about to flourish green once more.
                              Each instant's
worth both itself and its suspension –
its own infinity, conceivable florescence.
Such is time's blossoming in time,
and keeping time, each moment just
about to be – lips closed which part
and let so slowly arias unfold.

Those harmonies depend
on strife and reconciliation,
on agony, on joy,
on every quiver in the soul
plus change of self when scooping out
its own appropriate centre for itself.
Desire arises not from lack
or absence but that sudden call
from what's becoming to accomplishment.

Daniele Serafini
(1952–)

A Distant Venice *(Venezia lontana)*

In memory of Carlotta Z

'And somewhere at the bottom he fell into darkness. That much he knew. He had fallen into darkness. And at the instant he knew, he ceased to know.'
— Jack London: *Martin Eden*

For you water proved
at first companionship
then destiny
lagoon and river
offering birth
then oblivion
your brief lifetime
darkened
beneath a bridge
one autumn still echoing
that change of mind
that scream for help
too late before the last
and fatal swirl of water.

You'd grown up wearing
sad smile and a look of pride
walking head high
between San Polo and the waterfront –
grave, sedate, those early
shadows already on your face.

You loved embroidery,
delicate fingerwork
uncompleted like words
that leave no trace,
sunsets over the Lido.

You loved with fierce
possessiveness –
isolated, isolating –
unable to decide
among your store of trinkets,
Flemish miniatures or the scores
of music never played.

Venice became the bitter season
soon a mere memory
forgotten later in the slow
inertia of those muffled rooms
close to the castle of Colloredo
haunted by the light
footsteps of the lovers
in that novel – your ghosts,
your nightly companions.

Then, unexpectedly,
the clash of arms,
a sneak attack, soldiers,
tears shed, exhausted horses,
days spent with wind and mud
then a fresh smell
of dairy-farms and wheat –
a string of villages
Melegnano, Crema, Ombriano –
ending up in poverty
at Romanengo.

Here, years of hard
earth, parched earth, a land
of mulberry-trees and solitude,
your sons, those silences, a distant Venice –
and through the smoke of burning stubble
a harsher feeling of life,
a hoarse lament about exile
reducing to sepia all
memories of pallid water,
canals, marshes, islands
like Pellestrina or Torcello,
the dome of San Giorgio Maggiore –
places gone so remote
just images and sounds
all shattered in the hollow
quality of grief.

But water summoned
like a duty,
as nursemaid, tyrant,
in that October
heralding the end.
And one day you no longer knew
whether it was a canal
or a lagoon which seized you
so ferociously –
the current dragging,
the whirlpool distorting,
the river offering
eternal future,
altering voice, eyes, fate
to light of pure redemption
from domes, from crosses,
from cramped familiar squares –

then peace at last
graveyard on San Michele
only the fluttering of marsh-birds
and the suspended beating
of your weakened heart.

Ryôta
(1718-1787)

samidare ya
aru yo hisoka ni
matsu no tsuki

would in fact trickle
down the page without a gap
between the symbols:

Harry Guest

Ryôta's Twilit Haiku

    is concise, blooming
to revelation softly
    with tesseræ to
    start with: *fifth / month / rain /*
there's / evening / secrecy / in /
    pine-tree / of / the moon.
    Japanese has been
described as mirror-language
    to our own and we've
    a fine example
in line three since *no* equals
    apostrophe s.
    Matsu means "pine" and
tsuki "moon" therefore, reading
    backwards, it's "the moon
    of the pine-tree" – i.
e. the satellite's captured.
    She's "the pine's moon" now.
    The fifth month's not May
In Ryôta's time a New Year
    starts in February.
    June's notorious still
for its oppressive rainy
    season when a glimpse
    of faint sky's well worth
waiting around for whether
    through branches or not.

"a twilit haiku".
You sense unending rain day
   after day then one
   late afternoon just
a thinning to the greyness,
   fewer drops. The dusk
   paradoxically
sieves the air lighter. A break
   in the cloud allows
   now (though stealthily)
the pale shining of the moon
   beyond one dark tree.

Six Word-Sonnets

1. Du Bellay: *'Heureux qui comme Ulysse . . .'*
2. Ronsard (1524-1585): *'Quand vous serez bien vieille . . .'*
3. Baudelaire (1821-1867): **Les Chats**

1. Roam!
   Learn!
   Turn
   home.

   My
   land
   banned.
   Why?

   Rome
   here
   though
   home
   so
   dear.

2. When
   young
   sung.

   Then
   grey.
   No
   beau.

   Stay!
   Give
   this
   vow:

   Live!
   Kiss!

   Now!

3. They
   sleep . . .

   stray . . .

   keep
   sleek . . .

   groom . . .

   seek
   gloom . . .

   dream.

   Eyes
   are
   star-
   size . . .

   gleam.

4. Baudelaire: *Recueillement*
5. Mallarmé: *'Victorieusement fui . . .'*
6. Rimbaud: *Voyelles*

4. Grieve?
   No.

   Eve-
   glow.

   Crowd
   So
   loud.

   Go!
   Shun
   light.

   Sun
   drowned.

   Night
   found.

5. Storm
   clouds
   form
   shrouds.

   Night
   there.
   Bright
   hair
   seen.

   Sky
   shows
   my
   rose-
   queen.

6. "A"
   night.
   Day-
   white
   "E".

   Bled,
   see
   red
   "I".

   "U"
   eau.

   "O"
   blue.

   Why?

101

Harry Guest

Quantité Inconnue

Ma peau frissonne quand tu parles

Tes yeux aux volets clos expliquent
Ces songes mouillés que j'ai faits

Te défaisant de mes mains mûres
Profil sur tes épaules nues
Tu feins de n'avoir pas compris
Ce que tu acceptais de faire

Ta bouche prescrit l'espérance
Bien en train quoique grisonnant
Je courtise ton corps à poil
Un doux relent croît de tes reins
L'herbe scintille de rosée

(translation of *Unknown Quantity* from
Arrangements; London: Anvil; Press Poetry, 1968)

Notes on the Poets

MAURICE SCÈVE (p. 11) discovered the tomb of Petrarch's Laura while a student at Avignon. In 1544 he completed his masterpiece *Délie*, 449 intricately composed *dizains* possibly hinting at his love for Pernette du Guillet who, like Louise Labé, was a member of Scève's school of poetry in Lyon, then a flourishing literary centre. However, Délie is an anagram of *L'Idée*, teasing the reader to wonder whether the woman addressed is a fiction. The introductory short poem is underlined by the ambiguous capital letters SOUFFRIR NON SOUFFRIR which lends these beautifully enigmatic poems another wary richness.

JOACHIM DU BELLAY (p. 16) was one of the most richly inventive members of the Pléïade. *L'Olive*, his first collection, published in 1549, derives from his cousin's name Olive de Sévigné. He was following Petrarch's use of "Laura/laurel" and the poems, wonderfully experimental *tours de force*, are not meant to be 'personal' or, indeed, sincere.

PHILIPPE DESPORTES (p. 17) included 'Les Amours d'Hippolyte' among his *Premières Oeuvres* dedicated to the King of Poland in 1573. Hippolyte here is the wife of Theseus not the son whom Phèdre loved in vain. She has tentatively been identified as Marguerite de Valois, sister of Henri III. Like Du Bellay, Desportes is concerned primarily with the charm of poetic invention and the reader is meant to identify with the experience, not a putative biography.

THÉOPHILE GAUTIER (p. 19) was a genuine Romantic up in the gallery, wearing the famous red waistcoat to show violent praise at the first night in 1830 of Hugo's dynamic play *Hernani*. This made the Classicists in the stalls rage right from the start, as the play began with an enjambement (spilling over to the next line). This was anathema to tradition. The young men looked down on the traditionalists yelling "A bas les genoux!" as their bald heads looked like so many naked knees. Gautier's poems, however, tended to be strictly organized. He prided himself on his cool, dispassionate and objective attitude to life.

PAUL VERLAINE (p. 23) named his first collection *Poèmes saturniens* (1866) in homage to Baudelaire, who had warned his readers that

Les Fleurs du mal was "un livre saturnien, orgiaque et mélancolique". Verlaine prefaced his book with a definition of those born under Saturn ("fauve planète") whose lives will be "bonne part de malheurs et bonne part de bile". Monsieur Prudhomme – the typical bourgeois – was invented by the caricaturist Henri Monnier.

The last poems ARTHUR RIMBAUD (p. 24) wrote leave readers to decide for themselves what they are about and to compare their relationships one with another. They contain, along with teasing humour, references to alchemy ("seasons" can go from black through white and yellow to the red which foretells the goal of gold – they can also imply the open air of nature as opposed to the comfort (or prison) of the castles), his affair with Verlaine, his fear of failure, his need to discover the answer to it all. As well as verse he wrote many prose-poems in the selection called *Illuminations*, painted plates. These plates were thought for a long time to be illustrations but, when he was in London, it has been discovered that Rimbaud admired the colours and scenes in pottery laid out for sale near where he was living so now there is a new dimension given to the word.

MARIE-LUISE KASCHNITZ (p. 45) was born in Karlsruhe in 1901. After writing two novels in the 1930s she began to write poetry. *Gedichte* (Poems) appeared in 1947, followed by further collections. A firm if unorthodox Christian, she produced short stories and radio plays, dying in Rome in 1974.

ROLF HAUFS (p. 47) was born in 1935. As well as poems, he has written novels, short stories and radio-plays. In 2003 he was awarded the Peter Huchel Prize.

The semi-surrealist poems by ROLF-DIETER BRINKMANN (1942-1975) (p. 48) are well known in Germany, as are his important translations of Frank O'Hara and other American poets. He was killed in a car accident after reading at the Cambridge Poetry Festival.

ANNE MOUNIC (p. 90) is a fine poet who also translates superbly much English and American poetry. She has written several beautiful novels, *récits* and *nouvelles* as well as many works of literary criticism, including books on Robert Graves, Edwin Muir and Ted Hughes. She lectures at the Sorbonne and co-edits the splendidly thick literary magazines *Temporel* and *Peut-Être*. She is also a painter and an engraver.

DANIELE SERAFINI (p. 93), born in 1952, graduated from Bologna University in 1980. His poetry collections are *Paesaggio celtico* (1993) which was a finalist for the Diego Valeri Prize; *Luce di confine* (1994); *Eterno chiama il mare* (1997) which gained an honourable mention at the Eugenio Montale International Prize; and *Dopo l'amore* (2004). His short novel *Café Hàwelka* appeared in 1995 from Mobydick, Faenza, which has published all his work.

He is Head of the Museum Services in Lugo near Ravenna and Curator of the Francesco Baracca Museum of Aviation. He has edited the poetry magazines *Origini* and *Tratti* and translated many poems from French and English. His own work has been translated into several European languages.

Printed by BoD˝in Norderstedt, Germany